CLASSIFIED

SECRETS YOU'RE NOT SUPPOSED TO KNOW

BUSINESS AND BIG DATA

Influencing Consumers

Ellis Roxburgh

LUCENT PRESS

Published in 2019 by
Lucent Press, an Imprint of Greenhaven Publishing, LLC
353 3rd Avenue
Suite 255
New York, NY 10010

For Brown Bear Books Ltd:
Managing Editor: Tim Cooke
Designer: Lynne Lennon
Children's Publisher: Anne O'Daly
Design Manager: Keith Davis
Editorial Director: Lindsey Lowe
Picture Manager: Sophie Mortimer

Picture Credits
t=top, c=center, b=bottom, l=left, r=right
Interior: 123RF: prykodov, 16; AAP: 5b; Alamy: NetPhotos3, 29; Chicago Tribune: Antonio Perez, 33; iStock: alexsl, 7, AplamayoPhoto, 19, baona, 4, Erikona, 5t, Fentino, 45, FLDphotos, 34, fotokon, 20, GA161076, 35, Ellsaveta Ivanova, 8, JasonDoly, 32, Oktay Oryakcloglu, 18, monsitj, 1, 12, Rawpixel ltd, 23, wdstock, 21, yhelfman, 4; Public Domain: Amazon, 15, Apple, 40, Luca Fredia, 36, Geniron Biolabs, 39, Kevin Morgan, 41; Shutterstock: 2p2play, 31, BravoKiloVideo, 10, Dan74, 43, Ken Durden, 9, Emilio100, 42, J2R, 26, katz, 37, Olivier Le Queinec, 24, Felix Lipov, 25, mazlarz, 27, Macrovector, 11, MADSOLAR, 17, NanamiOu, 28, REDPIXEL.PL, 13.
Front Cover: (background) Shaun Jeffers/Shutterstock.com; (foreground) SThanaphat/Shutterstock.com.

Cataloging-in-Publication Data

Names: Roxburgh, Ellis.
Title: Business and big data: influencing consumers / Ellis Roxburgh.
Description: New York : Lucent Press, 2019. | Series: Classified: secrets you're not supposed to know | Includes glossary and index.
Identifiers: ISBN 9781534564329 (pbk.) | ISBN 9781534564305 (library bound)
Subjects: LCSH: Big data--Juvenile literature. | Data protection--Law and legislation--United States--Juvenile literature. | Privacy, Right of--United States--Juvenile literature.
Classification: LCC QA76.9.B45 R69 2019 | DDC 005.7--dc23
Manufactured in the United States of America

CPSIA Compliance Information: Batch #BS18KL
For further information contact Rosen Publishing, New York, New York at 1-800-237-9932

CONTENTS

CHANGING BUSINESS

Technology is revolutionizing the way businesses operate. That is having an effect on all of us as consumers.

Business is changing. For centuries, businesses have produced goods or services, and used advertising and marketing to encourage consumers to buy them. At the start of the 21st century, computers, online shopping, and social media have enabled businesses to find out far more about their **consumers**. In turn, this allows them to target individuals even more effectively.

>> Shopping Mall For businesses, individual consumers are sources of data that help shape their future plans.

>> Analysis
Modern businesses rely on new technology to analyze their performance.

>> Multinational
Companies such as McDonald's operate in many countries around the world.

Change is affecting all areas of business. In the financial sector, for example, it has become clear that economic problems can spread rapidly around the world, as happened in the global financial crisis of 2008. Meanwhile, the rise of multinationals (companies that operate in more than one country) presents a challenge to national governments. Where should these companies pay taxes, and which country's laws should they follow?

BIG DATA

Many businesses today are collecting huge amounts of information about their customers and their competitors. This information is known as "big data."

The type of data that makes up big data varies widely. Some is **demographic** data. This includes people's names and addresses, as well as information about how many people live in particular neighborhoods or cities. Other data is financial. It relates to people's income, expenditure, level of borrowing, and so on. Retail data analyzes people's shopping habits and their behavior on online retail websites. Other forms of data are related to transportation, health, and education. There is also information about social media use. This includes people's likes and dislikes, and what types of stories encourage users to click links to visit other websites.

The sources of big data also vary. Some comes from public records, such as health or social security information. Some comes from retail activity, where the patterns of customers' purchases are recorded in credit-card transactions or through the use of **loyalty cards** or points schemes. A major source of information is the Internet. Retailers track customers' online browsing to figure out what people might eventually buy.

>> Data Streams
Keystrokes on computers, traffic flow, and electricity usage are all forms of big data.

FAST FACTS

WHAT IS BIG DATA?

The term "big data" originated in the 1990s. It refers to data that is usually stored electronically in collections of millions of samples. Traditional methods cannot analyze so much information, but powerful computers can be programmed to extract patterns and identify trends.

FOR AND AGAINST

The way big data works reflects a theory called the Wisdom of Crowds, proposed by Francis Galton in 1907. Galton said that if you asked enough people a question and averaged out their answers, you would get an answer close to the correct one. Some people say that the approach only works for problems in fields such as math, and not more widely.

Search engines can also trawl through posts on social media to locate key words that reveal what users think about particular subjects. This might help to identify a trend in what customers are likely to buy in the near future.

>> Crowd Sourcing Everyone is the source of hundreds of pieces of data every day.

MANY USES

Big data is a potentially powerful tool. Instead of testing the reaction of dozens or hundreds of customers or potential customers, it means that businesses can analyze millions of individual pieces of data to try to identify patterns.

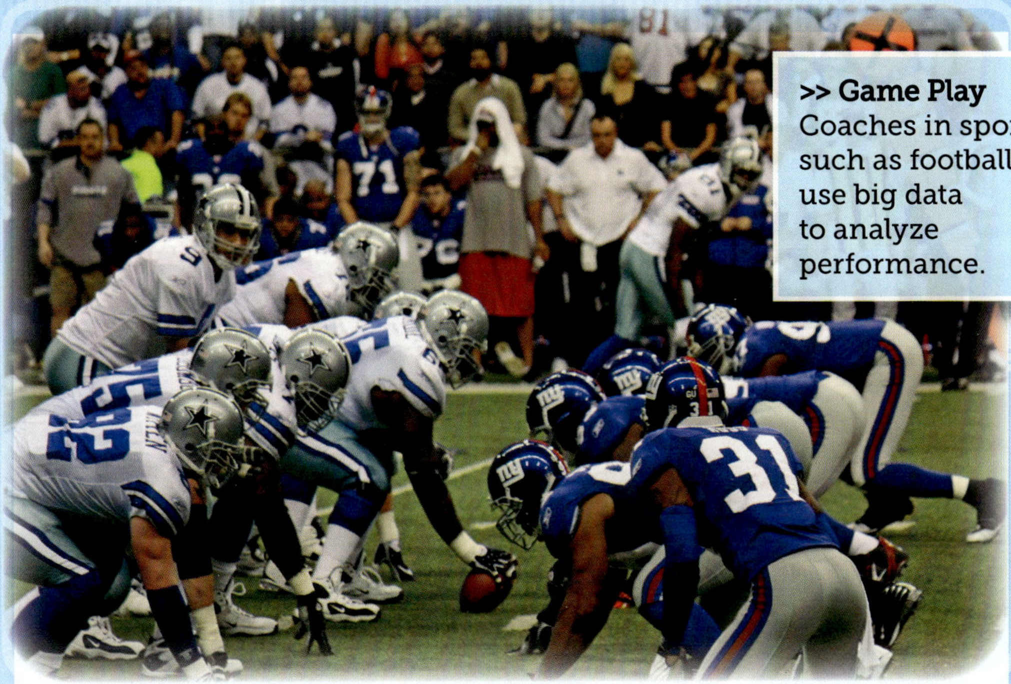

>> Game Play Coaches in sports such as football use big data to analyze performance.

The same ability to distinguish patterns and anticipate trends makes big data useful for many organizations, such as governments, media groups, and sports teams. Governments can use past behavior of citizens to anticipate future needs such as drug supplies. Broadcasters can learn in real time how social media users are reacting to their programs. Sports teams can analyze each movement of their own players or opposition players to figure out strengths and weaknesses, and compare games to thousands of other games.

There are other potential uses, too. Political parties and polling organizations can estimate approval or disapproval ratings for particular policies. Meanwhile, retailers can target customers with offers that reflect the previous buying history of millions of other purchasers.

>> Consumers Information about shoppers' habits is simply random data until it can be put together, sorted, and analyzed to figure out useful patterns.

STORAGE AND ANALYSIS

In order to use big data effectively, however, it is not enough simply to collect a lot of data. Businesses have to make sure that they can not only store the data on their own secure servers, but also that it is held in **databases** in such a way that it can be searched in various ways in order to identify patterns, **anomalies**, or parallels. Retrieving information from the database is done using either a commercially available computer program or a customized program specifically created for an individual business. This process is usually known as data mining.

The process of analyzing the data to try to acquire useful information is again carried out by computer. Human analysts would not be able to deal with the amount of information involved.

Big data is supported by a physical **infrastructure** of databases and servers. As consumers link up appliances in their home to the Internet, for example, information from those appliances is fed into central servers. That allows patterns to emerge not from the behavior of individual households but thousands or millions of households. This should help so-called **smart homes** make more efficient decisions in the future.

>> **Linked In** Appliances in smart homes are linked to central networks known as the Internet of Things.

WHAT DO YOU THINK?

Big data will help power the rise of the smart home. In a smart home appliances, such as central heating and the fridge, would run themselves. They would send data about the householder's behavior to a central database, which will help individual homes make smarter decisions about, for example, when to turn up the heating. But would you be happy about your data being used in such a way?

LANGUAGE ANALYSIS

Distinguishing patterns from data held in databases is only part of big data. Traditional, or classical, computing finds it difficult to deal with spoken languages. Computers are coded in a language of symbols, all of which are then converted into computer code that has only two characters: 0 and 1. These computer codes tell the **microprocessors** at the heart of computers how to behave. However, a technique known as natural language processing (NLP) has been developed as a means to extract usable data from information written in normal language.

>> Data Processing
Computer scientists are developing new ways to analyze business data.

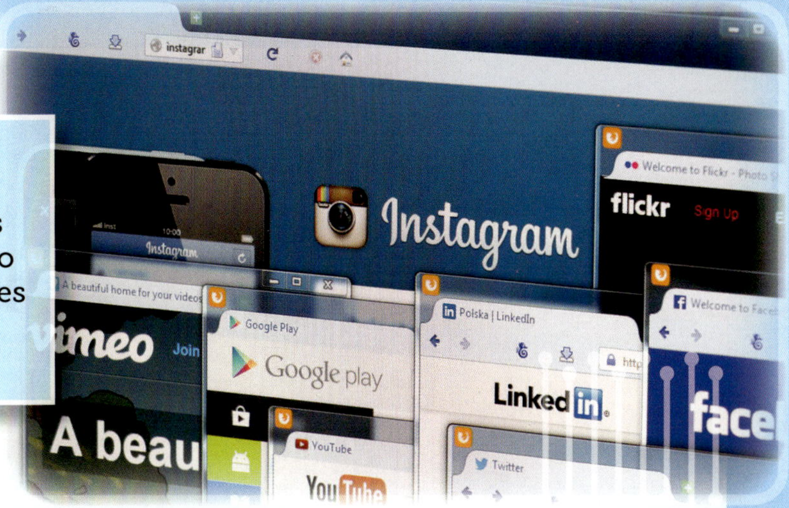

>> Trends
Social media gives retailers an insight into the preferences of millions of individuals.

NLP can trawl through entries on social media sites such as Facebook, for example, and identify expressions of positive feeling toward particular products or ideas or negative feelings against them. This allows human interactions on social media sites and message boards, or any public forum where people exchange ideas, to become the source of further information for big data.

NATURAL LANGUAGE PROCESSING

Developing computer programs that can work with normal language has challenged computer scientists for over four decades. The tasks involved include figuring out the differences in words that have more than one meaning, or that can be both nouns and verbs. It also includes detecting if someone is using humor, something that is difficult for a machine to recognize.

MARKETING AND RETAIL

Marketing and retail are leading the way in using big data and data analysis for business decisions. Retailers are using the technology to figure out the best way to put products and offers in front of the people most likely to buy them.

Retailers have access to data from various sources, such as loyalty schemes and credit cards. The first loyalty programs began in the United States in 1896, when the retailer S&H began to issue Green Stamps to its customers that they could trade in for bargains. In 1978, following **deregulation** of the airline industry, airlines such as American and United began to issue their own loyalty cards that travelers used to gain discounts and upgrades. This began the modern wave of loyalty cards and store cards. Retailers use loyalty cards as a source of information, allowing them to track the purchases of individual customers. Similar information is collected from people who use credit cards, either in store or online. Unlike cash, cards allow retailers to identify and analyze an individual's purchase history.

>> Robots Large firms such as Amazon have **automated** their warehouses, where red robots move around shelves of goods.

FAST FACTS

RETAIL OPERATIONS

Retailers sell goods to consumers, either in stores or online. Their business is based on predicting what customers will want, making it available, and pricing it to ensure maximum profits. Retailers use advertising to promote particular goods. Marketing is a broader effort to promote a retailer's identity, or brand, as being positive and trustworthy.

Online shopping is also a source of information for retailers. They can identify what people look at and find out what products are bought together. Retailers use this information to send the online browsers tailored suggestions of other products in which they might be interested.

CHANGING RETAIL

Leading retailers such as Walmart are investing in software that will process millions of transactions. Such programs will figure out buying patterns and the best way to make suggestions to potential customers. Some systems use **global positioning system** (GPS) technology to send messages to consumers driving or walking near a particular store. In the future, retailers hope to track customers as they walk through a store, directing them in real time toward offers likely to appeal to them.

Data analysis is also helping retailers make their operations more efficient.

>> Card Payment
Retailers can tell what online customers look at and for how long.

SUPREME STORY

The skater apparel store Supreme made its name by selling lines for only a brief time. Fans wanted to get ahold of rare items. Supreme released new lines online once a week. The clothes sold out in minutes. Teenaged entrepreneurs in Florida built a bot that jammed the site, ensuring that the bot could make the first orders. The teenagers then charged people to order Supreme clothing through them. Supreme objected, but the bots were not illegal so it could not stop them.

>> **Supreme Store** The first store opened in New York. This store is in Fukuoka, Japan.

Analysis of online **commerce**, for example, has revealed that many customers select products and put them in their shopping baskets, but pull out of making purchases at the last moment. Analysts suspected that this might mean they had mislaid their credit card details. In order to avoid losing sales in this way, the Swedish e-commerce site Klarna introduced a feature for the thousands of retailers it represented. This allowed customers to continue with the checkout without paying at the time. Instead, they received an **invoice**, to be paid later. The websites reported a fall in the number of sales abandoned at the last minute.

FOR AND AGAINST

Some retailers believe that online deliveries will soon be made by **drones.** Amazon, Google, and UPS are among the businesses developing such programs. They say they will be economical and convenient, and will take vehicles off the roads. Other people worry that the skies will become too crowded, with inevitable accidents.

>> Air Delivery Although numerous businesses have tested drone delivery, in 2017 no such services were operating.

USING DATA

Examining buying habits in different regions, retailers can figure out potential demand for products. Their distribution networks can ensure that adequate stores of goods are available in different parts of the country.

Another role of big data in retail is in making sure prices are right. One way retailers do this day to day is to collect and analyze data about the prices their competitors are charging.

They then set their own prices accordingly. However, big data is also leading to more significant changes in how shops price their goods. In the past, stores normally sold products at full price for a certain length of time. As demand fell or new lines were introduced, stores traditionally discounted the former goods dramatically in end-of-season or clearance sales. Now, retailers such as the department store chain Stage Stores use data analysis to identify the moment demand for a product begins to fall off. It then manages a more gradual reduction of prices. This has proved 90 percent more effective in selling off stock than the traditional approach.

>> Price Reduction
Data analysis may allow stores to avoid traditional end-of-season sales.

>> **Fashion Change** Fashion retailers such as Zara in Europe use technology to change their lines as often as every week.

BIG DECISIONS

Data analysis enables stores to order specific products or to develop specific lines, such as a new toy based on a trend in children's books and TV shows toward, say, dinosaurs. It also helps retailers to make more significant decisions. For example, the famous Macy's department store in New York City appeared to be trading well in the early 2010s. However, analysis of its customers suggested that Macy's was failing to attract younger shoppers, so-called **millennials**. The store realized its **customer base** would eventually shrink. In October 2015, Macy's opened a new basement named One Below to appeal to younger customers.

Identifying trends is supported by a process called sentiment analysis. This uses NLP to analyze social media streams to try to figure out general trends in how people feel—whether they are positive or nervous about the future. Retailers hope to turn this information into more opportunities for sales.

WHAT DO YOU THINK?

When Macy's in New York tried to attract younger shoppers, it opened a basement named One Below that was very different from the main store. The basement had a stand that allowed shoppers to select their ideal fitness assistants by using a computer interface. It also had a 3D printer that allowed customers to design and print their own cell phone cases, and an embroidery station where shoppers could have their jeans custom-embroidered. Do you think this kind of personalized shopping will become more normal in the future?

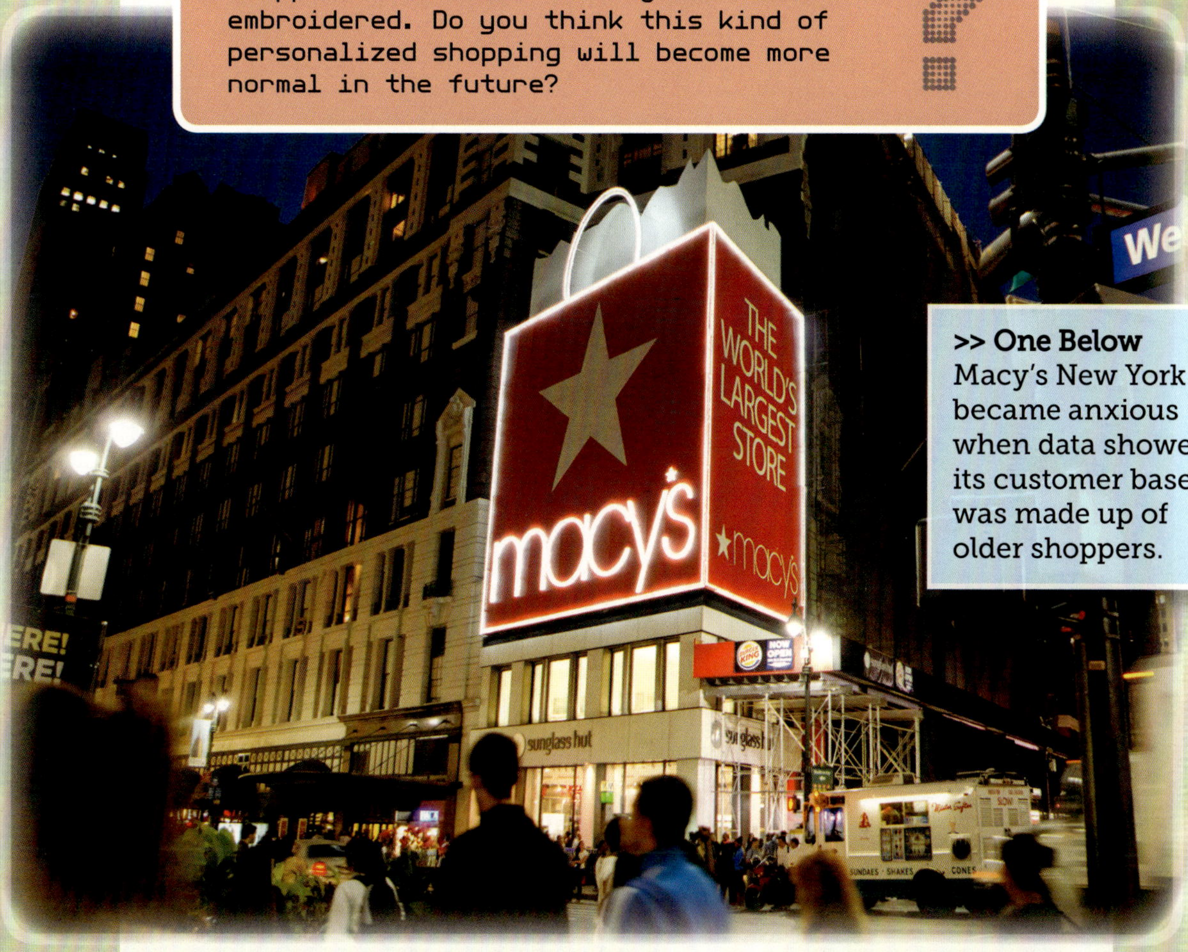

>> One Below
Macy's New York became anxious when data showed its customer base was made up of older shoppers.

FINANCE AND FRAUD

In the modern world, finance operates on a global scale. Businesses around the world are linked in a way that can have unexpected consequences.

The high degree of **globalization** in the financial world became clear in 2008, when a global crash began. The crash reflected a new degree of complexity in relations among financial institutions and in financial products and services. The crisis began in the United States, where institutions made increasingly risky loans. This type of lending is known as subprime loans, because the borrowers came from low-income groups to which lenders are traditionally reluctant to provide money. There is a higher chance that the lender will not be able to repay the loan and will **default**. However, subprime loans have a high **interest rate**, so if they are repaid the lender can make big profits. On a subprime **mortgage**, a lender can always take possession of a property and sell it. Banks and finance companies bundled together subprime mortgages and sold them as packages to other financial institutions.

CLASSIFIED

FAST FACTS

FINANCIAL SERVICES

Financial services include activities such as banking and insurance provision. They also include asset management, which is mainly concerned with investing pension funds. Venture capital is another area of finance. It generates funds to invest in business development and new businesses. Private equity is the management of wealthy individuals' **assets**, savings, and investments in companies.

>> Data Bank
Financial markets use technology that can update price rises and falls in fractions of a second.

>> Foreclosure In 2008, more than 800,000 American families lost their homes when they failed to pay their mortgages.

When many Americans began to default on their subprime mortgages, a wide range of institutions began to suffer. They included the well-known U.S. mortgage associations known as Fannie Mae and Freddie Mac. However, the effects of the defaults spread much farther.

GLOBAL CRASH

The biggest casualty of all was Lehman Brothers investment bank, which closed on September 15, 2008. After that shock, more U.S. institutions went bust or were bailed out by the government. The problem spread rapidly through the international economy. In Europe, banks collapsed and governments became involved in large-scale attempts to stabilize their economies. In Iceland, the three major banks in the country collapsed. Governments around the world took control of banks to guarantee the money they held. They injected large amounts of cash into the economy. By the end of 2009, the economic situation was stabilizing, but there had been considerable financial and political costs.

WHAT DO YOU THINK?

In 2016, 11.5 million secret records were leaked from Mossack Fonseca, a law firm based in Panama. The records revealed the secret financial dealings of many prominent figures. They had conspired with Mossack Fonseca to hide money in trusts and fake companies. The Icelandic prime minister, Sigmundur David Gunnlaugsson, resigned when it became clear he and his wife had invested money in a company that paid few taxes. Most of those exposed by the leaks argued that what they had done might have been unethical but not illegal. Do you agree?

For some observers, the financial crash was the result of poorly judged lending. For others, it was a warning that international finance had become so complicated that not even the people who worked in it understood it. The subprime market had led to firms around the globe owning assets whose risks they did not understand. The interconnected nature of banking, in which millions of transactions are carried out by computer networks, only made the problem spread quicker and farther.

>> Headquarters
Around 25,000 employees lost their jobs when Lehman Brothers collapsed.

>> **Car Sales** New finance deals allow people to buy cars—without ever paying the full cost.

CAR FINANCE

In the mid-2010s, some observers worried that a similar problem was building up in the world economy with the growth of subprime debt in car finance. In order to encourage people to buy new cars, finance agencies in the United States and Great Britain were permitting purchasers to set up personal finance deals called personal contract plans (PCP).

FOR AND AGAINST

Bitcoin is a so-called cryptocurrency, which means that it exists only online. There are no physical coins. It was created in 2009 and is now accepted by a growing number of merchants. The transactions are recorded by computer, without any human input. Some people think this is the way forward. They say there is no more risk in cryptocurrencies than in real currencies such as the dollar. Others say that cryptocurrencies are a bubble that will inevitably burst.

A PCP allows a customer to pay only a fraction of the car's value. The consumer can walk away at any time simply by returning the car, which then becomes the problem of the finance agency. In 2016, personal car loans in the United States totaled over $1.1 trillion.

BANKING FRAUD

Some observers worry that the increasingly complex financial market allows more room for fraud. This might take place at a corporate level, such as the **manipulation** by a group of bankers in the City of London of the rate at which banks loaned money to one another. The London Interbank Offer Rate (Libor) changes daily, and bankers colluded to change it in order to increase their profits.

>> City of London Bankers manipulated the lending rates for about 20 years before they were exposed in 2012.

PERSONAL FRAUD

More fraud takes place at a personal level. The rise of online banking has led to fears of an increase in fraud. A huge industry has developed around trying to guarantee the safety of both customers and the banks themselves. Some banks issue users with special card readers that generate digital codes to allow users to sign in to their accounts. One consequence of online banking is a decline in alternative payment methods, such as checks. Although checks remain popular in the United States, they are no longer used in many countries, and their use has dropped dramatically in other countries, such as the United Kingdom.

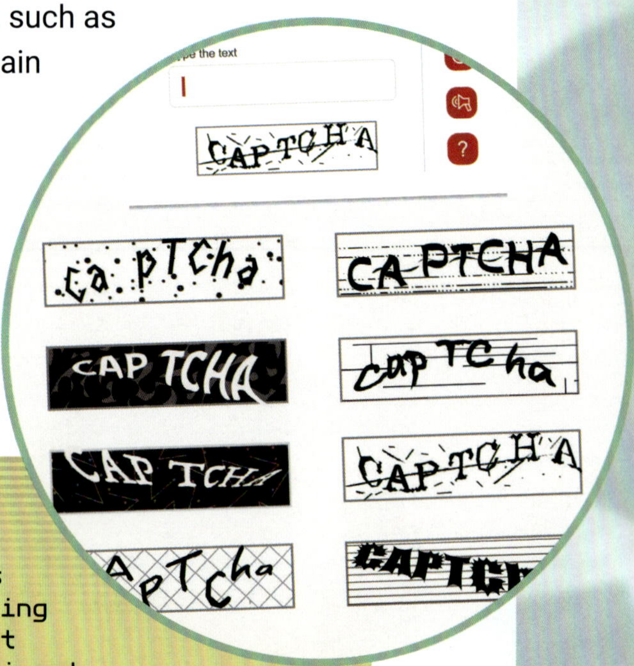

TOP SECRET

One way electronic businesses try to prevent fraud is by using Captcha. This is a system that asks a user to recognize and input a series of distorted letters and numbers to prove that they are human. The idea is that a machine will not be able to recognize the characters correctly. However, in 2017 programmers claimed that they have taught automated bots to identify the slanted and fuzzy letters.

>> Online Banking Internet banking is convenient—but is it also more open to fraud?

There are concerns that online banking and retailing leaves personal accounts open to criminals who hack the details in order to steal money. In a type of fraud called **phishing**, criminals send emails that appear to come from an individual's bank, asking for details of bank accounts. They even set up fake websites that look like genuine sites to try to get people to input their banking details. Another way criminals get access to people's bank accounts is by cloning, or copying, bank cards that are used in automated teller machines (ATMs). The criminals copy details stored in the magnetic strip on the backs of the cards.

Banks are spending millions of dollars to try to protect themselves and their customers from fraud. The criminals are usually one step ahead, however. The best defense against personal fraud remains individual vigilance by the consumer.

MULTINATIONALS

One business development that is set to continue in the 21st century is the rise of multinational companies. These are businesses that operate in more than one country.

Multinationals are not new. The first multinationals were the trading companies set up by Europeans in the 1600s and 1700s to exploit new discoveries around the world, from the Americas to Asia and the Pacific. The Dutch East India Company, for example, set up trading stations in what are now Indonesia, India, Japan, Taiwan, Malaysia, Thailand, Vietnam, and South Africa.

Modern multinationals emerged in the 20th century with the rise of oil companies that operated in many countries, such as Royal Dutch Shell and BP (British Petroleum). The spread of such companies was often closely linked to European and American **colonies** overseas. In the **post-colonial** world, manufacturing companies such as Nestlé and the Ford motor company also began to build bases in numerous countries, despite having a headquarters located in a specific country or city. They found it more profitable to manufacture products in a particular region rather than exporting products from the original factories, or they found it cheaper to use local labor and products.

>> Gasoline In 2017, the oil firm Royal Dutch Shell operated in more than 70 countries, including here in Thailand.

FAST FACTS

TYPES OF BUSINESS

A multinational corporation is a business based in one country that operates in more than one country. It usually has **subsidiaries** in these countries. A transnational corporation has no real home base. Another type of company, known as a stateless or cosmopolitan company, has a moving legal headquarters. It moves around to take advantage of taxation and other laws.

>> Online Companies such as Google that have offices in a few countries but operate in many countries are a new type of multinational.

At the same time, service industries such as banking became more multinational as a reflection of the increasingly global nature of the world economy. The improvement of communications—first radio and telephone technology, and later the rise of computers and the Internet—meant that it was no longer important where a bank or stockbroker was based.

A NEW BREED OF RETAILERS

A similar process occurred in the retail industry. Firms such as McDonald's, Starbucks, and Gap rolled out stores not just across the country but across the world. In 2015, McDonald's had 36,000 outlets operating in more than 100 countries. Online retailers such as Amazon and Apple operate in virtually every country, and shoppers can choose to purchase from whichever national site gives them the best deals.

FOR AND AGAINST

Many companies have chosen to outsource jobs. For example, sneaker manufacturers might move their operations to East Asia, where labor and materials are cheaper. This keeps the price of the sneakers cheaper, which benefits the consumer. However, it also leads to a loss of jobs in high-cost economies, such as the United States. Which matters more: low prices for consumers or high domestic employment?

>> Protest March Workers in Chicago protest a 2017 decision by the food manufacturer Nabisco to move production to Mexico.

The latest wave of multinationals has been led by giant technology companies such as Google and Facebook. They are different from most previous multinationals in that they do not have any physical product and do not need a physical base. The content of Google is distributed in servers all over the world but also in a non-physical virtual world that is not subject to national **jurisdiction**.

QUESTIONS OF TAXATION

The changing nature of multinationals raises many challenges for governments. One question is where they should be taxed and what laws they should be subject to. So-called stateless companies move their headquarters to take advantage of lower tax rates.

>> Facebook Boss Mark Zuckerberg agreed in 2017 that his site had a duty to monitor illegal content.

WHAT DO YOU THINK?

Technology businesses such as Facebook, Reddit, and Google claim that they are not traditional publishers. Therefore, they say, they should not be taxed in the same way as media organizations and publishers who create editorial content. They also argue that they are not responsible for the content of their sites, such as hate speech or propaganda for terrorist organizations. Do you think such businesses are responsible for the content they display?

>> Worldwide Starbucks operates in more than 50 countries. This café is in Kagoshima, Japan.

In the early 2010s, a series of scandals raised many questions about the tax payments of multinationals, including Amazon, Google, and Starbucks. They paid taxes in their home countries rather than in the countries where they made their money. Starbucks, for example, opened its first UK coffee shop in 1998. Over the next 14 years, it had UK sales worth £3 billion. However, it paid only £8.6 million in **corporation tax**, despite the tax rate being officially around 20 percent. In 2015, after a scandal about tax avoidance, Starbucks changed its policy. That year, it paid £8.1 million tax on its profits of £34.2 million—nearly as much as in the previous 14 years.

EXPLOITATION

The rise of multinationals is part of the globalization process. Business often now operates on a worldwide level. People in favor of globalization see it as part of the development of economic systems beyond national boundaries. For opponents, globalization is a sinister development. They say it allows corporations to avoid government restraints such as safety laws by relocating operations to countries with fewer restrictions. It has led to tragedies such as the Bhopal disaster in India in 1984, for example. A gas leak at a plant run by the U.S. company Union Carbide killed 2,259 people.

>> Memorial A painted memorial in India promises to pursue justice over the Bhopal disaster.

DISASTER

The Union Carbide pesticide plant at Bhopal in India was owned by an Indian subsidary of the U.S. multinational. On December 2, 1984, it became the site of the world's worst industrial disaster. A gas leak killed more than 2,250 people that night. More than 558,000 suffered ill effects from the leak, of whom around 16,000 later died. The Indian government blamed the disaster on poor management by Union Carbide. In 1989, Union Carbide paid $407 million to settle lawsuits related to the disaster.

>> New York Marchers in New York City at the start of the Occupy movement in 2011.

Globalization is also criticized for allowing manufacturers such as Adidas and Reebok to make products in countries where wages are much cheaper. This encourages the rise of sweatshops, where people work in harsh conditions for low wages. It also takes jobs away from economies such as the United States, where labor is relatively expensive.

PROTESTING GLOBALIZATION

In 2011, the Occupy movement emerged. Over the next five years, the movement staged protests against globalization in cities from New York to London and Hong Kong. Protestors objected to the fact that multinational companies operated without government restraints, and that governments were allowing them to do so. For protestors, this meant that firms were no longer paying attention to the responsibilities they believe all businesses should have to the communities in which they operate, and whose lives they help to shape.

INDUSTRIAL ESPIONAGE

Industrial espionage uses illegal methods to gather information about competitors to gain a commercial advantage.

There has been a long history of companies trying to benefit from their competitors with the aim of performing better. Sometimes, this is overt. If Apple launches a new tablet or iPhone, for example, engineers at other technology firms may purchase the new products in order to take them apart and learn new techniques and innovations. This runs the risk of breaking **copyright** law, but such law-breaking can be difficult to prove.

In the fashion business, too, designers usually work in great secrecy to prepare a collection, which is launched with a runway show during Fashion Week. However, almost as soon as a new look is revealed, more commercial retail firms begin to produce much cheaper versions of it for sale through department stores and other low-price outlets. In this world, in other words, being copied is the unavoidable risk of releasing a new product.

>> Biotech New fields such as biotechnology are vulnerable to espionage as new techniques are constantly introduced.

FAST FACTS

R&D

Most companies try to expand their business. They invest large sums of money into research and development (R&D) in order to develop new products and services. In fields such as biotechnology, pharmaceuticals, or computing, research can take years and cost millions of dollars. This is why companies guard the process closely, and why their competitors use espionage to try to find out about it.

Other attempts to gain an advantage are not illegal. They include studying the actions of other companies and trying to anticipate new developments in the market. This can be achieved simply by reading the business press or company reports.

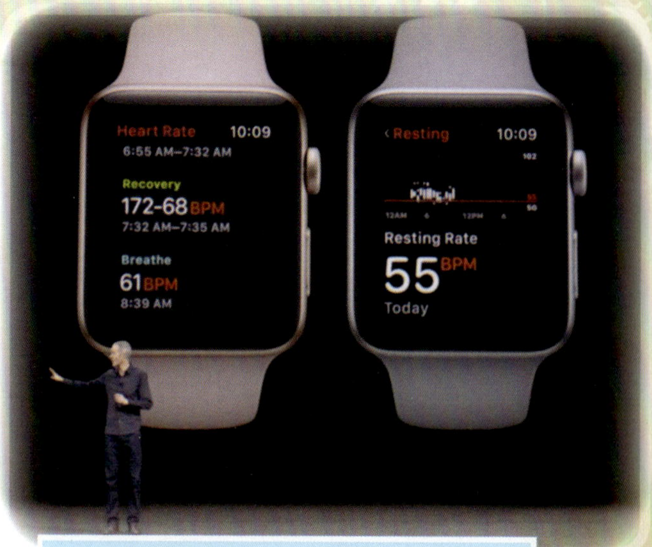

>> New Watch Anyone can buy a product after it is released. However, in theory they are forbidden from copying it by copyright laws.

Some attempts to learn about what competitors are doing use illegal methods such as fraud to try to learn information that other companies want to keep secret. These might be the details of new products, technological developments such as new components for machines, a planned **strategic** launch, or even alterations to prices. For competitors in the same marketplace, learning about what a company is about to do before it becomes public might give them a chance to get in ahead of the competitor or get ready to follow them.

SOURCES OF INFORMATION

Most industrial espionage is carried out by individuals who work for the company whose secrets are being stolen, or their suppliers and contractors. These people are **bribed** to pass on information or may have a grudge against their employer.

FOR AND AGAINST

One form of industrial espionage is for companies to spy on their own employees, monitoring their email traffic and even listening in to phone calls. Employers say this is necessary to ensure that workers are doing their jobs properly. However, many people claim that this is a breach of people's civil rights and right to privacy. Does the fact that a company is paying someone give it the right to monitor communications like this?

>> Hot Cars The automobile industry has historically been subject to significant amounts of industrial espionage.

In some forms of industrial espionage, a company hires individuals from another company, who bring their expertise with them. In 1993, the German car maker Volkswagen (VW) hired a team of executives from its rival Opel, part of General Motors. A legal case in 1997 forced VW to make a payment to Opel, as well as committing to buying parts from Opel for a period of seven years. In a similar move in 2009, the hotel company Hilton hired executives from a rival firm called Starwood. Starwood complained that Hilton had done this to learn about its plans to develop high-end luxury resorts.

>> Cosmetics
A competitor alleged that L'Oréal tried to steal its business secrets.

CARS AND MAKEUP

Industrial espionage has traditionally affected industries in which there is little basic difference among products, such as automobiles or cosmetics. In such competitive markets, any small advantage can help business. Car makers, for example, go to great lengths to disguise a new model during the long process of testing before it is released. They paint cars in camouflage to disguise their outlines or even strap on fittings to change their shape. In 2017, meanwhile, the French cosmetics company Guinot accused its rival L'Oréal of sending agents into its properties disguised as maintenance operatives to gather information. These operatives studied papers on people's desks and even looked through wastebaskets. L'Oréal denied the accusations.

WHAT DO YOU THINK?

One of the most secretive areas of sport is Formula 1. Every tiny technological development that might gain a car a fraction of a second is a closely guarded secret. In 2007, the Ferrari team accused two of its engineers of passing information to their rivals. The teams who had received the information said they did not use it. Neither the engineers or the teams were severely punished. Do you think they should have been?

>> Silicon Valley The software and technology center is a hive of industrial espionage as companies try to steal secrets.

ONLINE INDUSTRIES

The rise of the Internet has changed the nature of industrial espionage. First, new technology itself has become one of the businesses in which industrial espionage is most common as firms try to gain an advantage in a very competitive field. Second, Internet technology enables people to try to gain industrial secrets by hacking into computer systems.

GOVERNMENT HELP

Governments are sometimes involved in industrial espionage. National intelligence agencies gather information from businesspeople or students who have studied overseas. If the agencies learn anything important, they can pass it on to companies working in their own country. Better-performing businesses lead to a stronger national economy.

TOP SECRET

>> Carbon Copies Chinese firms often release their own versions of Western websites. Baidu is the Chinese version of Google.

Industrial espionage like this may involve governments trying to gain an advantage for their economies. In 2010, Google reported that operatives inside China had been using Google and Microsoft to hack into the accounts of foreign companies working in China. The operation was probably carried out with the knowledge of the Chinese government. That same year, the US company CyberSitter took the Chinese government to court for stealing some of its programs. The original programs had been developed to stop children from looking at unsuitable Internet sites. The Chinese wanted to use it to limit all access to the Internet, as part of a project known as the Great Firewall of China, which seeks to prevent free access to online content.

ONGOING PROCESS

Like big data, Internet espionage seems likely to grow. In an increasingly global world, businesses are eager to find any advantage they can over their competitors. It is simply the latest development in the long struggle to gain more customers and raise business profits.

GLOSSARY

anomalies Facts or events that deviate from what is normal or expected.

assets resources with economic value.

automated Performed by a machine.

bribed Dishonestly persuaded to do something, usually by a cash payment.

colonies Areas governed by a home country.

commerce The activity of buying and selling, particularly on a large scale.

consumers People who buy goods and services for their own use.

copyright Laws that protect someone's intellectual property.

corporation tax A tax applied to the profits of a business.

customer base The people who repeatedly buy things from a store or use particular services.

databases Information stored in a way to make it easily accessible using a variety of search criteria.

default To fail to keep up repayments on a loan.

demographic Related to the population.

deregulation A reduction of the rules that apply to a particular business.

drones unmanned aerial vehicles that fly without pilots.

global positioning system (GPS) A navigation system that uses satellites to pinpoint locations on Earth.

globalization The process by which businesses operate on a wide international scale.

infrastructure The physical apparatus needed to keep systems running.

interest rate The cost of borrowing money.

invoice A demand for payment.

jurisdiction The geographical area in which particular laws apply.

loyalty cards Cards that allow consumers to gain rewards by using firms frequently.

manipulation Controlling something for your own advantage.

microprocessors Small processing circuits inside computers.

millennials People reaching adulthood in the early 21st century.

mortgage A loan made in order to allow someone to buy real estate.

post-colonial Describes the world after the end of Europe's empires in the mid-20th century.

phishing Illegal attempts to gain financial information online.

smart homes Homes in which appliances run themselves.

strategic Relating to long-term business plans rather than short-term goals.

subsidiaries Companies controlled by another company.

FURTHER RESOURCES

Books

Carr, Aaron. *World Trade*. Global Issues. New York: Av2 by Weigl, 2014.

Eboch, M. M. *Big Data and Privacy Rights*. Essential Library of the Information Age. Minneapolis, MN: Essential Library, 2016.

Freedman, Jeri. *When Companies Spy On You: Corporate Data Mining and Big Business.* Spying, Surveillance, and Privacy in the 21st-Century. New York: Cavendish Square, 2017.

Wolny, Philip. *Understanding Financial Frauds and Scams.* Real World Economics. New York: Rosen Publishing Group, 2012.

Websites

www.american-historama.org/1990-present-modern-era/2008-financial-crisis.htm
A history of the 2008 financial crash in the United States.

www.bbc.co.uk/schools/gcsebitesize/geography/globalisation/globalisation_rev1.shtml
Pages from the BBC about the process of globalization and what it means for all of us.

www.capella.edu/rio/it-hub/analytics-careers/big-data-and-analytics/
A page from Capella University with examples of data analytics in action.

www.fwthinking.com/videos/future-big-data-video.htm
A page from How Stuff Works with a video about the use of big data.

Publisher's note to educators and parents: Our editors have carefully reviewed these websites to ensure that they are suitable for students. Many websites change frequently, however, and we cannot guarantee that a site's future contents will continue to meet our high standards of quality and educational value. Be advised that students should be closely supervised whenever they access the Internet.

INDEX